BUDGET SURVIVAL GUNS

MW00397515

HOW TO BUILD AN ARSENAL OF FIREARMS FOR PERSONAL DEFENSE AND DISASTER PREPAREDNESS WITHOUT BREAKING YOUR BANK

Ronald Williams

© 2017

Ronald Williams Copyright © 2017

All rights reserved. No part of this book may be reproduced in any form without permission in writing from the author. Reviewers may quote brief passages in reviews.

Disclaimer

No part of this publication may be reproduced or transmitted in any form or by any means, mechanical or electronic, including photocopying or recording, or by any information storage and retrieval system, or transmitted by email without permission in writing from the publisher.

While all attempts and efforts have been made to verify the information held within this publication, neither the author nor the publisher assumes any responsibility for errors, omissions, or opposing interpretations of the content herein.

This book is for entertainment purposes only. The views expressed are those of the author alone, and should not be taken as expert instruction or commands. The reader of this book is responsible for his or her own actions when it comes to reading the book.

Adherence to all applicable laws and regulations, including international, federal, state, and local governing professional licensing, business practices, advertising, and all other aspects of doing business in the US, Canada, or any other jurisdiction is the sole responsibility of the purchaser or reader.

Neither the author nor the publisher assumes any responsibility or liability whatsoever on the behalf of the purchaser or reader of these materials. Any received slight of any individual or organization is purely unintentional.

Thank You For Downloading!

Before we start I would like to thank you for downloading this book of mine.

My biggest passion in life is sharing the experiences and knowledge I have accumulated over the years with others, so it means a lot to me that you've decided to take time out of your day to read it.

As a gift, I have an additional book for you that you might like.

Normally I sell this book for $2.99 on Amazon, but you can have it for FREE by subscribing to my mailing list.

In joining my mailing list, you'll also become instantly notified of when a new book of mine has been published and given a free promotion day on the Kindle Store, so you can get each new book I publish for free as well.

CLICK HERE TO SUBSCRIBE

Thank you!

TABLE OF CONTENTS

INTRODUCTION

Hi there, I would like to thank you for downloading this book "Budget Survival Guns." I hope you find what you are looking for and receive value from it!

Do you want to buy a gun or multiple guns but are constrained by a tight budget? If so this guide is for you!

One of the most important aspects of any survival or disaster preparedness plan is security. In fact, security should be one of your main priorities along with food and water. After all, what good is assembling a stockpile of supplies if you don't have the capabilities to defend it?

This is why it's important to own guns (and ammunition) as part of your survival stockpile. You need guns to defend your home and your family from those who would harm you, and to put food on the table should you need to hunt.

The problem here, of course, is that you may be on a tight budget while knowing full well that guns aren't cheap. Fortunately, I'm here to tell you that can purchase high quality guns without breaking your wallet.

Now you may believe that by buying cheaper guns you're sacrificing quality. While it is definitely true that there are a lot of cheaply made and unreliable firearms out there, it's also true that there are a lot of high quality guns out there for cheap prices as well.

Firearm manufacturers know full well that not everybody has mountains of cash to spend, which is why for the last few years they've begun producing high quality guns at a lesser price point. It's these guns that I want to talk about today.

What I want to do with this book is outline the basic categories of guns you need for disaster preparedness and then go over specific makes and models of guns within those categories that you can have without spending a fortune.

The specific subjects that we are going to cover include:

- Types Of Guns You Need In Your Arsenal
- Budget Pistols
- Budget Revolvers
- Budget Shotguns
- Budget Rifles
- How To Build An Arsenal For $500, $1,000, and $1,500

Now if you're already an expert on firearms in general, then this book probably won't be for you.

But if you're a beginner and you realize that owning guns is important for the safety of you and your family, then you've definitely come to the right place.

I'm going to teach you how you can put together a complete arsenal of firearms that will be easily affordable for most people, and thus hopefully affordable for you too.

Let's get started!

Types Of Guns You Need In Your Arsenal

Before we dive into the specific makes and models of budget guns that are out there, it would probably be wise to establish the specific categories of guns that you need first, right?

Let's briefly go over the basic categories of guns that you should have in your survival arsenal:

.22 Rifle

A .22 rifle is truly a class of its own, and no gun collection of any kind is truly complete without one. Even though the .22 caliber is fairly light for self-defense (though it could be used in that manner if intended), it's still easily one of the most versatile firearms that you can own.

You can use a .22 rifle for the following purposes:

- Small Game Hunting
- Target Practicing/Plinking
- Varmint/Pest Control
- Introducing New People To Shooting
- General Homestead Use

Another advantage to the .22 is how light and small the ammunition is. You can literally carry hundreds of rounds of .22 in the same amount of space that you could only carry a few dozen rounds of another caliber.

In addition, since .22 has minimal noise and recoil, it's literally the perfect caliber for introducing new people to shooting with.

Is a .22 rifle the single most important firearm you can own? That's certainly up for debate, but no one can deny that it is certainly one of the most important. Later in this book, we'll discuss specific makes and models of budget .22 rifles for you to consider.

Shotgun

A very strong and compelling case can be made that the shotgun is the single most important firearm to own. There's good reason for this argument.

With a shotgun, you can go bird/small game hunting with birdshot, big game hunting with slugs, and use it for home defense with buckshot rounds.

There is simply no other category of firearm in the world that provides you with this kind of amazing versatility.

I specifically recommend that you go with a pump action over a semi-automatic purely for reliability reasons. While there are reliable semi-auto shotguns out there, they are higher priced and any of the lesser priced ones are more finicky. Pump actions, in contrast, will feed literally anything you give them.

Handgun

Next up is a handgun. I would actually argue that the handgun is the single most important firearm that you should own simply because you can conceal it on your person. This reason alone will prove to be very advantageous in certain scenarios.

The handgun, however, should never be thought of as a primary weapon. Rather, it is a secondary weapon (or sidearm) that you keep strapped to your hip so you can present it in a moment's notice. Think of it as the weapon that you use to fight your way to your rifle rather than your primary armament, for instance.

When choosing a handgun, you will always have a fundamental choice between a semi-automatic pistol and a revolver. Both have their upsides and downsides. Semi-automatic pistols, though more complicated, hold lots of bullets (at least with double stack models) and are faster to reload.

Revolvers, in contrast, have limited capacity but are far simpler in operation. Almost anyone can learn how to pick up and shoot a revolver within seconds, whereas a semi-auto pistol is just a tad more complex for people.

Personally, I feel that the semi-automatic is superior. For situations where you're up against multiple attackers, having more bullets in your gun and the ability to reload quicker is highly desirable and potentially lifesaving.

But that's just me. You may prefer to have a revolver if you desire something simpler, or you can have both if you want as well.

We'll go over examples of budget semi-automatic pistols and revolvers later in this book.

Centerfire Rifle

Finally, the last category of gun you need in your arsenal is a centerfire rifle. I probably should have split this up into two separate categories (defensive rifle and hunting rifle), but since you're on a budget, we'll just keep it at one.

At the very least, you need a centerfire rifle that can tap targets at long distances and put food on the table. A simple lever action or bolt action rifle would suffice here.

I also believe in the importance of owning a semi-automatic defensive rifle (such as an AR-15 or AK-47) as well, but remember, we're speaking on budgetary terms here so owning a semi-automatic rifle may not be realistic if our budget is tight.

Take note that you can use one center fire to fulfill different roles. For example, a lever action rifle makes for a great hunting tool while also being an adequate defensive weapon as well (you can fire and load a lever action far faster than you can a bolt).

In summary, the four categories of guns you need in your arsenal are:

- .22 Rifle
- Shotgun
- Handgun
- Centerfire Rifle

For the next few chapters in this book, we'll outline and discuss specific makes and models of pistols, revolvers, shotguns, and rifles available for you to buy.

Afterwards, we'll go over how you can build a complete arsenal on separate budgets of $500, $1000, and $1,500 respectively.

Budget Pistols

In this chapter, we'll go over specific makes and models of semi-automatic pistols that are both high quality and affordable. Each of the pistols we are about to go over come from reputable manufacturers, are currently being produced at the time this book is being written, and are regularly priced at $400 or less.

Here are the budget pistols I recommend, presented in alphabetical order:

Bersa Thunder 380 (Price: $250-300)

Are you familiar with the famous Walther PPK pistol? If so, then you'll definitely notice its resemblance to the Bersa Thunder 380.

First of all, yes, this is a .380 caliber pistol and is much weaker than the 9mm. Some firearms experts would not recommend the .380 as a primary defensive caliber. Nonetheless, I'm throwing the Thunder 380 in the list just because of the incredible value it represents.

Priced at only $250-300 (and sometimes less than that), the Thunder 380 is an steel framed DA/SA auto. The steel frame means this gun is heavy, but that also means recoil is very manageable and makes accurate follow up shots easily.

The weapon features a slide mounted safety/decocker lever; when the lever is depressed, the safety is engaged and the hammer safely drops to the double action position at the same time.

Another great advantage of the Thunder 380 is how concealable it is. In scenarios where concealment would be very beneficial, the Thunder 380 makes for a very attractive option.

Standard magazine capacity on the Thunder 380 is 7 rounds, but 8 rounds magazines are also available from Mec-Gar (a high quality aftermarket supplier of magazines). In addition, a model called the Thunder 380 Plus is available that holds 15 rounds.

Bersa Thunder Pro (Price: $400)

The next offering from Bersa we will take a look at is the Bersa Thunder Pro. No, not the Thunder 380, the Thunder Pro.

This is a steel framed full size service handgun available in 9mm (17 rounds) and .40 S&W (13 rounds). Compact versions of both handguns are available as well, in addition to a .45 compact version (but not a .45 full sized).

The Thunder Pro features a frame mounted safety/decocking lever and is like the Thunder 380 a DA/SA weapon. This means the first trigger pull is long, while all subsequent shots are short. Once you decock the weapon, it returns to the long trigger pull for safer carry.

The Thunder Pro is currently in service with a number of South American militaries and law enforcement agencies. All in all, it's a decent value and has proven itself to be a reliable and rugged handgun.

Canik TP9 (Price: $300-330)

If you were to ask me what the overall best value is for a handgun on the market right now, I would have to say the Canik TP9.

Canik is a Turkish firearms manufacturer who are currently being imported into the United Sates by Century Arms. They are essentially clones of the Walther P99 pistol (a most excellent firearm but also higher priced), and subsequently are very reliable and accurate handguns.

Even though Canik is a recent company, their guns have gained a small but dedicated following due to their low prices and high quality. The TP9 currently consists of a number of different pistols including the TP9SA, TP9SF, TP9SF Elite, and the TP9-V2.

Each of these Canik pistols are excellent for a home defense or SHTF sidearm. Standard capacity in each pistol is 18 rounds for the full size model, but magazines are still interchangeable with the 15-round Walther P99 and PPQ magazines.

Another reason why the Canik pistols represent such an extraordinary value is because their guns are sold as kits: in addition to the pistol itself, you also receive an extra magazine, a paddle/belt holster, a mag loader, and a cleaning rod.

All in all, I highly recommend any of the Canik Tp9 pistols. If you're looking for an utterly reliable and high capacity handgun, I can't think of anything else that beats it.

Ruger 9E (Price: $250-300)

Next up is the Ruger 9E, a budget version of Ruger's own SR9 pistol. The SR9 is a polymer framed striker fired 9mm handgun with a double stack magazine, and was marketed as the thinnest such pistol on the market.

I actually prefer the 9E over the SR9 because the SR9 has an ugly looking flap that extends out of the top of the slide when the pistol is chambered, but the 9E doesn't have this.

The SR9 is essentially identical to the SR9 and is therefore fully compatible with SR9 17 round magazines and holsters. However, a few differences exist. Most notably, the finish on the 9E is not quite as good as the SR9 and will wear easier, but this is to be expected with a lower priced pistol.

The Ruger 9E also features a frame mounted safety on the frame, which some new shooters may find desirable.

Just before, I mentioned that nothing else beats the Canik TP9 (at least in my opinion) for a high quality and high capacity semi-automatic pistol. So what do I not like about the 9E in comparison to the Canik?

The answer is the magazine disconnect. A magazine disconnect is a safety feature on certain pistols meaning that the weapon will not fire when no magazine is inserted. I don't like this feature because I believe a true defensive handgun should still fire a single round out of the chamber without a magazine needing to be in the weapon.

The SR9 also features a magazine disconnect but it is removable; in the 9E, it unfortunately is not.

Overall though, the 9E represents a great value. Brand new, it's very easy to find them for the $250-300 range, and Ruger is a highly reputable company that has been around for a long time. So long as you are willing to have the magazine disconnect on your pistol, I would suggest that you give the 9E a look.

Smith & Wesson SD9/SD40 (Price: $250-300)

Another pistol offered at practically the same price as the Ruger 9E and from another highly reputable manufacturer is the Smith & Wesson SD9 in 9mm (or its .40 S&W counterpart the SD40). The SD9 holds 16 rounds of ammunition while the SD40 holds 14 rounds).

The SD-series is a development of Smith & Wesson's previous Sigma series of handguns. While the Sigma series was a failure by almost all accounts, the SD represents a significant upgrade and the quality matches Smith & Wesson's flagship but more expensive M&P line.

The SD9 and SD40 are highly reliable weapons that will eat any kind of ammo you put through them. However, they have one significant downfall to be aware of: the trigger.

The trigger pull on these guns is long and mushy to say the least, and that makes firing several follow up shots accurately a little more difficult in comparison to competing designs.

Fortunately, it's nothing that you can't fix. There are a variety of aftermarket triggers for the SDs that are much crisper and lighter and that you can have installed by a gunsmith, but out of the box, the trigger on the SDs is not very desirable.

It is predominately for this reason that I do not recommend the SD9 or SD40 has highly as I do the Canik Tp9. But overall, it's still a great value and will serve you well as a defensive firearm.

Taurus Millennium PT111 G2 (Price $200-250)

Next up is the Taurus Millennium PT111 G2 in 9mm (as well as its .40 S&W counterpart the PT140 G2).

The PT111 G2 is a compact pistol that holds 12 rounds of 9mm ammunition (or 10 rounds in the case of .40 S&W). It has become quite popular in the United States due to the fact that it is small enough to conceal and yet large enough to get a full grip on to fight with.

The PT111 G2 features an ergonomic grip that's been stippled so you can easily grip it even when your hands are wet. It also features a frame mounted safety on the side of the frame.

As a DA/SA pistol, the PT111 G2 features restrike capability. This means if you pull the trigger and hear a 'click,' you can pull the trigger again in an attempt to fire the weapon again instead of having to rack the chamber. This could be a lifesaver in a life-or-death situation.

The PT111 G2 also comes installed with Taurus' Security System, which is a lock on the gun that will disable the entire weapon if the lock is turned with a key provided. This is either a positive or a negative depending on how you see it. It's a positive if you want to store your gun away knowing that a burglar or a child will not be able to fire it in the event they find it, but that could also be a negative if you need to use your gun defensively only for the lock to be engaged.

Overall though, you're getting a lot of gun for your money with the PT111 G2. Even brand new, I've seen these guns for just $199 (though $200-250 is more common). If you're looking for a budget compact pistol that you can easily conceal while also being large enough to fight with, I'd give it a serious look.

Taurus PT92 (Price: $375-400)

Another gun worth mentioning from Taurus is the PT92 in 9mm. This is a clone of the famous Beretta 92FS pistol, which has been in service with the U.S military since 1985 (though is currently being phased out in favor of the Sig P320).

However, a few differences exist between the PT92 and the 92FS, with the most notable difference being the safety. The 92FS has its safety and decoking lever on the slide, while the PT92 has it located on the frame, which is much more convenient and easy to reach.

In addition, the safety and decocking positions on the PT92 are separate. Flip up to put the gun on safe, and flip down to decock it. This permits cocked and locked carry (single action mode with the safety on), unlike the 92FS.

You might be wondering why the PT92 is lesser priced than the Beretta, which commonly runs at $600 or more new. Does this mean the PT92 is low quality?

Not at all. In fact, functionality and reliability wise, the PT92 and 92FS are on equal footing.

The reason why the PT92 is cheaper is due to the finish and the cheaper cost of manufacturing in Brazil. The finish on the PT92 is duller than the 92FS and will wear easier, but you can only expect this for a lower priced handgun.

The PT92 ships with 17 round magazines, though 18 round magazines are also available from Mec-Gar. As an all-steel pistol, it's heavy and large, but recoil is also kept to a minimal. This is a true service handgun and not a concealment handgun.

As with the PT111 G2, the PT92 also comes installed with Taurus' Security System. It also features a tactical rail for adding accessories such as lights or lasers.

Walther Creed (Price: $350)

The last budget pistol that we will discuss is from Walther, the Creed in 9mm. This is the most recent pistol in this list, but is still a great option for a home defense or SHTF sidearm.

Walther has become very well known for their highly ergonomic and comfortable pistols such as the P99, PPQ, and PPS. I personally own the PPQ and have found it to be the most ergonomic striker fired pistol on the market (at least in my opinion, and that's why I bought it).

The Creed is essentially Walther's budget pistol, and is a development of their previous PPX design. However, the ergonomics and stippling on the Creed is extremely similar to the PPQ. I would go as far as to say that the Creed is the most ergonomic handgun in this list.

The Creed is a DA-only hammer fired weapon, which differs from the PPQ's striker fired operation. This means the trigger on the Creed is not quite as nice as the PPQ's trigger (which is a dream to shoot, by the way), but it's still not at all bad for a budget priced handgun.

The Creed holds 16 rounds of 9mm ammunition in its magazine, and uses the same magazines as Walther's PPX (another budget pistol from Walther, but in my opinion it is inferior to the Creed in terms of ergonomics).

Overall, Walther makes great guns with high quality engineering. Their weapons have become known for their reliability and especially for their ergonomics, and even though it's their lower priced model the Creed fails to disappoint.

Budget Revolvers

Next, we'll discuss budget revolvers. As I noted earlier, I do prefer semi-automatic pistols due to their larger capacity and ease of reloading.

That being said, revolvers are certainly appealing due to their simplicity and ruggedness.

If you were to ask me what brand of revolver to consider if price were not an issue, I would straight up answer with Ruger and Smith & Wesson. The problem, as you may have guessed, is that Ruger and Smith & Wesson are higher end revolvers and are commonly sold at prices of $500-700 or more.

Therefore, sticking with budget guns under the $400 price range, here are the top budget revolvers I would suggest:

Charter Arms Undercover (Price: $300-330)

Charter Arms is a very successful manufacturer of revolvers who currently produce dozens upon dozens of different kinds of revolvers for the budget minded.

One of their most notable and popular models is the Undercover snub nosed revolver in .38 Special. This is a 5 shot compact revolver with a short 2-inch barrel, making it a perfect choice for concealment or as a backup weapon.

All Charter Arms guns are manufactured here in the United States, which is also pretty cool.

The reason why I specifically recommend the Undercover is because it is rated for +P .38 Special ammunition, a more powerful round than standard .38s but also a round that many other revolvers are not rated for.

In addition, so long as you are willing to spend $50-100 more, you can also go with an Undercover Lite model that is much lighter than the standard Undercover.

EAA Windicator (Price: $250-300)

EAA stands for European American Armory. Their Windicator revolver is a .357 Magnum that holds 6 rounds in the cylinder, and can therefore also shoot .38 Specials.

Overall, the EAA Windicator is a suitable choice for a budget revolver. They come in a variety of different barrel lengths and are certainly very affordable.

That being said, the Windicator also sports fixed sights rather than adjustable sights, and they have rough edges and tool marks on them as well (though this is arguably to be expected with such a low priced revolver).

Still, it's a revolver, which means the Windicator will give you the simplicity and reliability that you desire. For that reason, I recommend it.

Taurus 605 (Price: $275-300)

Taurus has been making firearms for the budget minded for some time now, and if you're looking for a snub nosed revolver, I would pay close attention to their 605 model.

While the Taurus Model 85 is a more popular snubnose revolver, the difference between the 85 and the 650 is that the 85 is a .38 Special while the 605 is a .357 Magnum.

.357 Magnum revolvers can also chamber and fire .38 Specials, but the same does not happen vice versa. Therefore, by choosing the 605 you have options, and options are good.

The .357 Magnum is certainly a powerful round and has gained a reputation as a one shot man stopper. It also produces hard recoil that will be undesirable to some shooters, and if you are such a shooter, you can just go with .38 Specials that are much easier to shoot.

Taurus 65 (Price: $350-400)

If you want a full sized revolver, the Taurus 65 represents a solid option with its 7 shot cylinder (rather than the standard 6). The 65 is also a .357 Magnum, so again, you have options between shooting .357 or .38.

There is a .38 Special model of the 65 called the 82, which is actually more popular, but again I don't see why you would go with a .38 model when you could just as easily purchase a .357 and then only shoot .38s through it anyway.

I would specifically recommend a Taurus 65 in stainless steel with a 4 inch barrel. A 4 inch barrel provides greater accuracy and velocity due to the longer sight radius than any barrel that's shorter, while also being easier to wield than a longer barrel.

Stainless steel is also much more rust and corrosion resistant than bluing, which is more desirable in unfriendly or wet conditions and requires less maintenance.

Budget Shotguns

For this chapter, we will discuss shotguns that you can buy for less than $400. I'm specifically going to stick to pump action shotguns because they are far more reliable than semi-automatics. Plus, the mere sound of the pump racking is sometimes enough to deter an intruder or at least to get them to think twice.

Here are the top budget shotguns that I recommend, again presented in alphabetical order:

Breech Loading Shotgun ($100-150)

Okay, I kind of lied a little when I said I was only going to focus on pump action shotguns. If you're on an extreme budget (and many people are), you can easily find a new or used single shot shotgun (such as an H&R or Rossi) in 12 Gauge for the $100-150 price range.

Even though you only have one shot before you need to reload, breech loading shotguns are still incredibly simple with very few moving parts. So from that perspective, they will last you a long time.

Maverick 88 (Price $200-225)

The cheapest shotgun that I could recommend is the Maverick 88 shotgun. This is a budget model of the Mossberg 500, another excellent shotgun that I will get to in a bit.

The Maverick 88 is regularly priced for the $200-225 range, though I have also seen new or used ones in good condition available for around $150-ish as well.

The Maverick 88 differs from the 500 in a number of aspects. For one thing, the 500 has a fully ambidextrous tang mounted safety while the Maverick 88 has a crossbolt safety that favors right handed rather than left handed shooters. This safety is also nonreversible, so if you're left handed the 88 is not going to that appealing of an option.

The Maverick 88 also has a different trigger group from the 500 and are only available in standard bluing, whereas the 500 is also available parkerized or in stainless steel (both of which are more rust resistant).

Something I will say before moving on is that when buying a shotgun, I recommend you get a model with both long and short interchangeable barrels. This way you can have a long 26-28 inch vented rib barrel for hunting and a shorter 18.5 inch barrel for self-defense.

Mossberg 500 (Price: $300-400)

Next up is the Mossberg 500, and though it's higher priced than the Maverick 88, it's still commonly available for less than $400.

The Mossberg 500 is currently the second most popular shotgun in the United States (the first is the 870), and as a result accessories and replacement parts are widely available.

The Mossberg 500 is a very user friendly shotgun, with an ambidextrous tang mounted safety on the back of the receiver, and a slide release lever located behind the trigger guard rather than in front of it like with the 870.

But the strongest testament to the 500 is how the military-spec 590A1 model is currently the only pump action shotgun to have ever passed the U.S military's 3443G torture test to be accepted into military service.

Overall, the Mossberg 500 is my personal preference for a shotgun due to its user friendliness and stout ruggedness and reliability.

Remington 870 (Price: $300-400)

The most popular shotgun in the United States is easily the Remington 870. Available for that same $300-400 price range as the Mossberg 500, the 870 has an absolutely limitless number of accessories, add-ons, replacement parts, and customization options available on the marketplace. There can be little doubt that the 870 is the AR-15 of the shotgun world.

The 870 is a very rugged and dependable shotgun with a smooth action (even though I personally prefer the Mossberg 500, I will concede that racking the slide on the 870 is smoother).

The 870 features a crossbolt safety on the rear of the trigger guard, while the slide release is located in front of the trigger guard. I personally find these positions to be slightly less user friendly than the Mossberg 500.

The 870 also has a steel receiver, while the 500 has an aluminum receiver that is lighter but also arguably not quite as durable.

Overall, the Remington 870 represents an outstanding choice for a shotgun for both hunting and home defensive use. It's not a shotgun that's going to let you down.

Winchester SXP (Price: $300-400)

The last budget shotgun that I'll discuss is the Winchester SXP. This is essentially a modern day development of the old Winchester Model 12 shotgun, which is still held in very high regard today.

The SXP, however, is easily distinguishable from the Model 12 due to its modern appearance, synthetic furniture, and aluminum alloy receive in comparison to the Model 12's steel receiver.

The SXP is not nearly as popular as the Mossberg 500 or Remington 870, which means that spare parts and accessories cannot be as easily located. Therefore, you might be wondering what advantage the SXP has over either of those two popular shotguns.

The answer lies in the pump action itself. The SXP utilizes an inertia assisted slide action that is far smoother and easier to rack than either the 500 or the 870. In fact, Winchester claims that it is possible to pump and fire three shots within half a second (though with enough practice, of course).

The SXP is available in a number of different variations and is offered at that same $300-400 price point as the 500 and 870. Overall, it's a great choice for a modern day all-around shotgun.

Budget Rifles

In this chapter, we'll discuss budget rifles. I'll divide this chapter into two sections. First, we'll discuss .22 rifles, and then we'll talk about centerfire rifles.

There are three specific budget .22 rifles that I recommend, which are in alphabetical order:

Marlin 60 (Price: $150-200)

First up is the Marlin Model 60, which is currently the second most popular .22 rifle in the United States (the first is the Ruger 10/22). This means that spare parts and accessories are very easy to find for the Marlin 60, and it's incredibly easy to customize as you see fit.

Numerous variants of the Marlin 60 currently exists. It feeds either 14 or 17 rounds in a tubular magazine underneath the barrel; the rounds must be fed individually, which is slower than simply swapping magazines. However, the lack of a detachable magazine also means that the rifle is very narrow and easy to store away and transport.

The Marlin 60 has a weight of five and a half pounds and is therefore easy to tote around. Overall, this is an excellent rifle for homestead use, plinking, and varmint control/small game hunting.

Mossberg 702 (Price: $100-150)

Need something even cheaper than the Marlin 60? If so, you'll want to take a look at the Mossberg 702. The 702 is actually manufactured in Brazil and then sold in the United States under Mossberg's name.

It feeds from standard 10 round magazine, but also accepts 25 round magazines. Its main appeal, besides its low price, is how lightweight it is at just four pounds. This is a superb rifle to teach a young child how to shoot, not to mention the lightweight means you yourself can pack it with you without hardly noticing that you even have it.

Overall, the Mossberg 702 is not my first choice for a .22 (I like the Marlin 60 and Ruger 10/22 more). But if you're on an extreme budget, it's a good way to go).

Ruger 10/22 (Price: $200-250)

My personal choice for a .22 rifle is the Ruger 10/22. This is without question the most popular rimfire rifle sold in the United States, and customization options and spare parts and accessories are literally limitless.

What you'll notice right away when you pick up the 10/22 is it doesn't feel like a toy. It feels like a true, rugged rifle, which is exactly what Ruger intended.

The 10/22 comes standard with 10 round rotating magazines, though I suggest that you upgrade to extended 25 or 30 round magazines instead for larger capacity. With that kind of firepower, the 10/22 could serve you well as a defensive weapon if needed.

Something else I will say is to take a look at the Ruger 10/22 Takedown. This is a variant of the 10/22 that easily breaks down into two separate pieces (the barrel and then the receiver/stock) and can be stowed away in a compact black bag that sells with the gun.

Overall, I believe the Ruger 10/22 is the finest .22 rifle ever made. It's accurate, reliable, rugged, dependable, and customization options are truly endless.

Now that we've gone over .22 rifles, let's next go over centerfire rifles for you to consider.

Here are the budget centerfire rifles I would recommend, presented again in alphabetical order:

Budget AR-15 (Price: $500-600)

Yes, there are AR-15s available for a relatively low price point. Even though $500-600 is higher than any of the other guns we've covered in this guide so far, that's still a decent price in the world of ARs where costs many times go over a grand.

Many manufacturers of AR-15s have begun producing budget or entry level rifles to choose on a tight budget or who are just getting into ARs.

The two budget AR-15s that I recommend the most are the Ruger AR-556 and Smith & Wesson M&P15 Sport II. The reason why I recommend these two AR-15s is because they come with a number of the same features that higher end AR's come with, such as a dust cover and forward assist.

Both Ruger and Smith & Wesson are highly reputable American companies, and you're definitely getting a lot of bang for your buck (literally) with either rifle.

The AR-15 itself is an excellent all-around platform. The 5.56x45mm NATO round it fires is sufficient for taking down deer, recoil is kept to a minimum, reloading is simple, and the velocity and stopping power is much better than that of a pistol. It is for these reasons that you will find the AR-15 to be a superb defensive weapon, especially against multiple attackers.

Not only that, but the AR-15 is also the most popular type of rifle produced in the United States. As a result, there is absolutely not shortage of spare parts, accessories, and customization options.

Mossberg 464 (Price: $350-400)

The Mossberg 464 is currently the best lever action rifle I can recommend for somebody on a budget. While I personally prefer the Winchester 1894 and Marlin 336, both of those (especially the Winchester) are regularly priced above $500 and therefore not the best option for someone without a lot of money to spend.

The .30-30 itself isn't a bad all-around rifle either. It's an excellent deer hunting rifle, and it can be used adequately for self-defense because it has a faster firing rate and reloading time than a bolt-action rifle. Lever actions are also very sleek and slender, so they take up very little space in storage or when you throw them into the back of your car.

The Mossberg 464 also provides you with a number of different features that make it well worth its value, including an ambidextrous tang safety, a recessed muzzle crown, a recoil pad, and an incredibly smooth action when working the lever.

Mossberg Patriot (Price: $300-400)

Another rifle option from Mossberg, though a bolt action, is the Mossberg Patriot. In fact, I believe that the Mossberg Patriot represents your overall best value for a bolt action rifle on the market currently.

The reason why is because the Patriot is available as a combo pack with a Vortex scope already pre-installed on the rifle (and Vortex has proven themselves to be an excellent optics manufacturer) while still being sold below a $400 price point.

The Patriot is also available in all major calibers and feeds rounds through a detachable box magazine, that allows ease of reloading. An adjustable trigger on the Patriot also allows you to make the trigger as light and as crisp as you desire.

Ruger American (Price: $300 to 400)

The Ruger American is a bolt action rifle that is noted for its rotating magazine that is similar to the 10/22's magazine. The American comes available in practically all major centerfire calibers (.270, .308, .30-06, 7MM, .300 Win Mag and so on), and also features an adjustable trigger that will be as light or as short as you desire.

Another desirable feature of the American rifle is its ambidextrous tang safety that is very easy to access, and the fact that it clocks in at a very lightweight six and a quarter pounds.

In summary, you have three primary types of centerfire rifles to choose from: semi-auto, lever action, and bolt action. For a budget semi-auto I recommend a Ruger AR-556 or Smith & Wesson M&P15 Sport II, for a budget lever action I recommend a Mossberg 464, and for a budget bolt action I recommend a Mossberg Patriot or Ruger American.

Each of these rifles provides you with excellent value and will serve you well.

Next, let's learn how you can build a complete arsenal for $500, $1,000, and $1,500.

How To Build An Arsenal For $500, $1,000, and $1,500

In this chapter, we'll discuss how you can put together a complete arsenal of firearms for a $500, $1,000, and $1,500 budget based on the guns that we've already gone over.

Building An Arsenal For $500

$500 is not a lot of money to spend on guns. You may believe that having just $500 to spend means you can only buy one gun.

But I'm here to tell you that you can have the three most critical guns you need (pistol, .22 rifle, shotgun) for just that amount. While you won't be able to buy any premium variations of these guns for $500, you can still buy completely dependable models.

Here are the following guns you can buy for a $500 budget:

- Taurus PT111 G2 9mm ($225) – personal defense, concealed carry, general purpose sidearm

- Mossberg 702 .22 Rifle ($150) – plinking, small game hunting, vermin control, introducing new people to shooting

- Single Shot Shotgun ($125) – home defense (buck shot), small game/bird hunting (birdshot), big game hunting (slugs)

Even though these may not be the most desirable firearms, they do cover all of your basic needs, and that's what matters. Remember, you only have $500 to spend here, and I think for that budget these three guns together represent your best options.

Building An Arsenal For $1,000

Let's say that you have $1,000 to spend instead of $500. We can now start to include some slightly higher priced guns.

Here are the guns you can buy for a budget of $1,000:

- Canik TP9SA/TP9SF ($300) – personal defense, concealed carry, general purpose sidearm

- Marlin 60 .22 Rifle ($150) -- plinking, small game hunting, vermin control, introducing new people to shooting

- Maverick 88 12 Gauge Shotgun ($200) – home defense, bird/small game hunting, big game hunting

- Marlin 464 .30-30 Rifle ($350) – medium to large game hunting, defense

With these four guns, your bases are again entirely covered.

These guns are essentially upgrades over the guns you could buy for $500:

- The Canik TP9 holds more rounds than the Taurus Millennium PT111

- The Marlin 60 is a better built gun than the Mossberg 702

- The Maverick 88 is an actual pump shotgun with a 6+1 capacity instead of the single shot shotgun

You'll also notice the inclusion of a centerfire rifle, the Mossberg 464. While you could just as easily go with a bolt action rifle such as the Mossberg Patriot or Ruger American here, I put the lever action on the list because it's better suited for defensive use (if it needs to be) than a bolt action.

As I mentioned before, lever actions carry more rounds, have a faster rate of fire, and shorter reloading times than a bolt action. Plus, the .30-30 Winchester is a very common and easy to find round, and a good choice for SHTF use.

Building An Arsenal For $1,500

Now let's say that you have $1,500 to spend on your survival arsenal. Here are the guns that I would recommend you have for this price range:

- Canik TP9SA/TP9SF ($300) -- personal defense, concealed carry, general purpose sidearm

- Ruger 10/22 .22 Rifle ($200) -- plinking, small game hunting, vermin control, introducing new people to shooting

- Maverick 88 12 Gauge Shotgun ($200) -- home defense, bird/small game hunting, big game hunting

- Mossberg Patriot .308 Rifle ($350) – big game hunting, long distance shooting

- Ruger AR556 ($550) – home/property defense, hunting

Okay, so we actually went a little over our initial budget, spending $1,600 instead of $1,500.

But the benefit here is that you really have all of your bases covered this time: you now have a sidearm, a .22 rifle, a shotgun, a hunting rifle, and a defensive rifle.

And you did it all by just spending sixteen hundred dollars (plus tax of course). What's better, is that each of the guns in this list are excellent models and will last you for a long time.

CONCLUSION

Thank you for reading this book! I hope you received value from it!

By reading this guide, you now know each of the basic types of guns you need to have in your survival arsenal and you also have a list of the specific makes and models of budget guns you can buy.

Again, I focused exclusively on guns that are both affordable and quality. There are many other excellent firearms out there as well, but because they cost more money, I didn't include them in this book.

The next thing for you to do is to keep this guide as a resource as you go about and begin to build your survival arsenal. I recommend that you buy one gun at a time and train specifically with that gun on the range before you move on to buying another one.

I also hope that you will pass on this guide to anyone else you know who is on a budget and wants to buy a gun so they can learn exactly what you have learned as well. After all, knowledge is something you want to pass on, not keep to yourself.

Good luck!

THANK YOU FOR READING!

CHECK OUT MY AUTHOR PAGE BY **CLICKING BELOW**

<u>AMAZON AUTHOR PAGE</u>

If you enjoyed this e-book, then please share your thoughts by leaving a review on Amazon!

Don't Forget To Subscribe!

Before you leave, I'd love to have you join my mailing list if you haven't already!

Remember, by subscribing to my mailing list two things will happen:

1. You will immediately receive A FREE PDF copy of a book I normally sell for $2.99

2. You will be notified every time I publish a new book and run a free promotion day on it, so you will be able to download every future book I publish FOR FREE as well

This is truly an incredible deal, so you don't want to miss out!

<u>CLICK HERE TO SUBSCRIBE</u>

Thanks!

Additional Books Of Mine

If you enjoyed this book, then I think you might enjoy these other ones I have written as well:

Bug Out Vehicle

Car Survival Kit

DIY Makeshift Weapons For Survival

Everyday Carry Guide For Survival

Family Prepping For Survival

Food Preservation For Survival

Situational Awareness For Survival

Survival Caches

Survival Myths

Trading Commodities For Survival

Underground Shelter For Survival

About The Author

Ronald Williams is an accomplished outdoorsman, survivalist, and survival writer whose passion is making sure that people are equipped with the knowledge and skills they need to outlast any kind of unexpected survival or disaster situation that comes their way.

Most importantly, Ronald wants to make sure that each person understands that disaster preparedness is a major responsibility to take not only for the safety of themselves, but for their friends and families as well.

Drawing upon both his extensive knowledge and his personal experiences, Ronald's books and articles have helped thousands of men and women across the globe learn how they can properly prepare themselves and their families for whatever unexpected disaster scenario comes their way to boost their chances of survival and ensure that they make it out alive.

Ronald has ghostwritten hundreds of articles on disaster preparedness for various reputable survival publications, including Off The Grid News.com, Survival Sullivan.com, Reloader Addict.com, Urban Survival Site.com, Survival Know How.com, and Legally Concealed.com.

When Ronald's not writing, he's usually camping, hiking, hunting, fishing, teaching others about survival and disaster preparedness, and spending time with his friends and family.

Made in United States
Orlando, FL
02 July 2023

34714476R00019